Philippa and the Dragon

Last week, a dragon came to our school.

He stomped into the classroom without even knocking.

Some children hid and some children howled.

But Philippa, quiet little Philippa, went on reading.

At playtime, the dragon followed everyone outside.

Some children hid and some children howled.

But Philippa, quiet little Philippa, went on jumping rope.

At lunchtime, the dragon roared, "I'm hungry!"

Some children hid and
some children howled.
But Philippa, quiet little Philippa,
shouted,
"STOP! I've had enough of you!"

The dragon stopped roaring.
He began to cry.
"I'm hungry, and no one will play with me," he sobbed.

Philippa smiled and gave the dragon a pat.
"Don't cry," she said.

"You can share our sandwiches.
Will you toast them for us?"

The dragon smiled.
"Toasted sandwiches coming up," he said.